Dog & Cat Frames

Frame photos of your favorite friends with man's best friend.

Dalmatian Frame

MATERIALS: 1½" x ⅛" flat wood disk • Woodsies: small heart, 2 medium teardrops, 2 medium eggs, 2 large eggs, 4 small rectangles • 4 jumbo craft sticks • Acrylic Paint: Lamp Black, Snow White, Santa Red • 12" of ⅛" Red satin ribbon • ¼" Black pompom • ¾" wood block • 3¼" x 4" piece of felt • Black permanent marker • Acrylic spray sealer

1. Cut craft sticks for basic frame and assemble. See diagram on page 2.
2. Paint frame and wood pieces. Sponge spots.
3. Glue wood pieces on frame. Glue felt on back leaving one side open for photo. Tie ribbon bow and glue. Glue wood block on back of frame for stand.

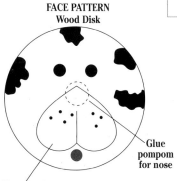

FACE PATTERN
Wood Disk

Glue pompom for nose

Glue small heart to head for muzzle

2. Paint frame and wood pieces.
3. Glue wood pieces on frame. Tie ribbon bow and glue. Glue felt on back of frame leaving one side open for photo. Fold chenille stem in half, twist together and glue folded end on back of frame for tail. Glue wood block on back of frame for stand.

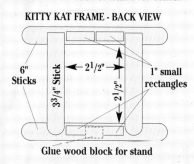

KITTY KAT FRAME - BACK VIEW

6" Sticks
3¾" Stick
2½"
2½"
1" small rectangles

Glue wood block for stand

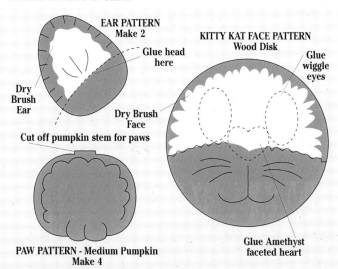

MY PAL

Dog House Frame

MATERIALS: 6 jumbo craft sticks • Woodsies: large angel, large heart, 2 medium ovals, 16 small hearts, 7 small rectangles, small circle, 3 small teardrops • 2 ¾" wood blocks • 7mm Black acrylic cabochon • Acrylic Paint: Green Mist, Cashmere Beige, Gingerbread, Snow White • Black permanent marker • 4" x 5½" piece of felt • Acrylic spray sealer

1. Cut craft sticks for frame and assemble. See diagram.
2. Paint frame and wood pieces. Glue wood pieces together and glue to frame. Glue cabochon for nose.
3. Glue felt on back leaving one side open for photo. Glue wood blocks on back of frame for stand.

EAR PATTERN
Make 2

Glue head here

Dry Brush Ear

Cut off pumpkin stem for paws

KITTY KAT FACE PATTERN
Wood Disk

Glue wiggle eyes

Dry Brush Face

Glue Amethyst faceted heart

PAW PATTERN - Medium Pumpkin
Make 4

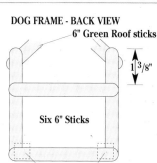

DOG FRAME - BACK VIEW
6" Green Roof sticks

1 ³/₈"

Six 6" Sticks

Glue wood blocks for stand

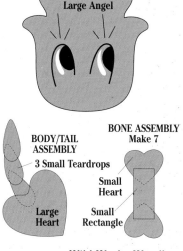

FACE PATTERN
Large Angel

BODY/TAIL ASSEMBLY
3 Small Teardrops

Large Heart

BONE ASSEMBLY
Make 7

Small Heart

Small Rectangle

Fun Character Frames

Match these adorable frames to

Freddy Fireman

MATERIALS: 1¾" x ⅜" craft disk • 4 jumbo craft sticks • ¾" wood block • Woodsies: 2 large ovals, 4 small rectangles • Jesse James buttons: 2 Yellow fire hydrant, Black star with Red center • Acrylic Paint: Lamp Black, Snow White, True Red, Mink Tan, Cadmium Yellow • 3⅜" x 3¾" and 3" x 5" pieces of Yellow craft foam • Pink and Black textile markers • Acrylic spray sealer.

1. Make basic frame on page 2.

2. Paint frame and wood pieces. Dry brush edges of boots and gloves.

3. Transfer and cut out patterns for hat from craft foam. Glue pieces together. Glue wood pieces to frame. Glue remaining foam on back of frame leaving one side open.

4. Glue wood block on back of frame. Glue fire hydrants on front of frame.

Happy Amber

MATERIALS: 1¾" x ⅜" craft disk • 4 jumbo craft sticks • Woodsies: 4 small rectangles, 2 large ovals • Acrylic Paint: Lamp Black, Snow White, Blueberry, Santa Red, Flesh Tone • 18" of 20 gauge copper wire • 4" of ⅝" White gathered lace • Eleven 2" strands of Red yarn • 2 Red 1" satin shoestring bows • ⅜" Red ribbon rose with Green ribbon leaves • 3¼" x 3⅝" piece of felt • ⅜" wood beads to spell name • ¼" wood beads • Twice as many 3mm Red beads as ¼" beads • Pink and Black textile markers • Acrylic spray sealer

1. Make basic frame on page 2.

2. Paint frame and wood pieces. It helps to stick beads on a toothpick while painting.

3. Glue wood pieces on frame.

4. Glue lace under chin. Fold and glue ends of lace on back of frame. Glue ribbon rose on collar and felt on back of frame leaving one side open.

5. For handle, string name beads and glue centered on wire. Coil wire around pencil. Shape handle. Wrap ends around arms. Secure ends. Glue handle on back of arms and Red satin bows on ends of arms.

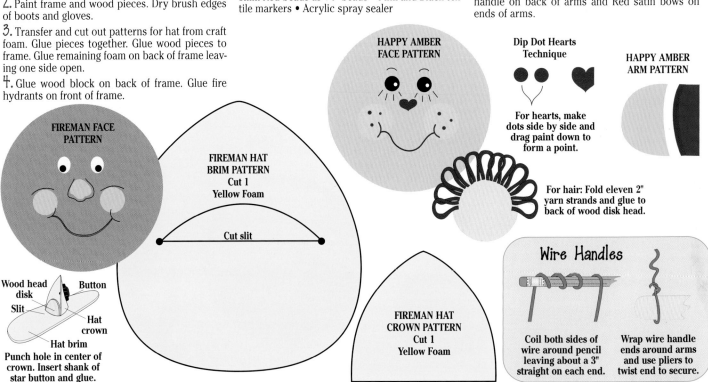

FIREMAN FACE PATTERN

HAPPY AMBER FACE PATTERN

Dip Dot Hearts Technique

For hearts, make dots side by side and drag paint down to form a point.

HAPPY AMBER ARM PATTERN

FIREMAN HAT BRIM PATTERN
Cut 1
Yellow Foam

Cut slit

For hair: Fold eleven 2" yarn strands and glue to back of wood disk head.

Wood head disk
Button
Slit
Hat crown
Hat brim
Punch hole in center of crown. Insert shank of star button and glue.

FIREMAN HAT CROWN PATTERN
Cut 1
Yellow Foam

Wire Handles

BUTTER

Coil both sides of wire around pencil leaving about a 3" straight on each end.

Wrap wire handle ends around arms and use pliers to twist end to secure.

your own little characters. From a cowpoke to a living doll, character frames are a hit with all.

Dandy Andy

MATERIALS: 8 jumbo craft sticks • 1½" x ⅜" craft disk • Woodsies: 2 large ovals, 6 small rectangles• Acrylic Paint: Lamp Black, Snow White, Blueberry, Santa Red, Flesh Tone • Nine 2" strands of Red yarn • 12" of ¼" Red satin ribbon • 4⅝" x 5⅞" piece of felt • Two ¾" wood blocks • Black and Pink textile markers • Acrylic spray sealer

1. Cut craft sticks for basic frame and assemble. See diagram.

2. Paint frame and wood pieces. Make dip Dot Hearts for nose and frame.

3. Glue wood pieces on frame.

4. Tie ribbon bow, glue below chin. Glue felt on back leaving one side open for photo. Glue blocks on back of frame for stand.

Flowery Jasmine

MATERIALS: 1½" x ⅛" flat wood disk • 5 jumbo craft sticks • Woodsies: 2 large ovals, 4 small rectangles • ¾" wood block • Acrylic Paint: Cadmium Yellow, Dark Chocolate, Lamp Black, Snow White, Pumpkin, Holly Green, Flesh Tone, True Red • 15" of 20 gauge copper wire • Three 8" strands of Black yarn • Three 9" pieces of ⅛" Yellow satin ribbon • 3¼" x 3⅝" piece of felt • Acrylic spray sealer

1. Make basic frame on page 2.

2. Paint frame and wood pieces.

3. Glue wood pieces on frame. Braid yarn leaving ¾" on each end. Tie ribbon bow on ends of braids. Glue braid to head. Make bow, glue below chin. Attach wire to arms. Glue name banner on front of wire, felt on back leaving one side open for photo and wood block on back of frame.

Giddy-up Cowpoke

MATERIALS: 1¾" x ⅜" craft disk • 4 jumbo craft sticks • Woodsies: small star, 2 large eggs, 4 small rectangles • Acrylic Paint: Lamp Black, Flesh Tone, True Red, Sapphire, Milk Chocolate • Turquoise 9mm x 6mm pony bead • 18" of 20 gauge Icy Silver wire • 9" of ⅛" Red satin ribbon • 3" x 5" of Black craft foam • ¾" wood block • 3⅝" x 3¾" piece of felt • 1" Brown feather • Pink and Black permanent markers • Acrylic spray sealer

1. Make basic frame on page 2.

2. Paint frame and wood pieces.

3. Glue all wood pieces on frame. Tie ribbon with bead around neck. Coil wire around pencil. Shape handle, wrap ends around end of arms and twist with pliers to secure. Glue handle on back of arms.

4. Transfer patterns for hat, cut from craft foam and assemble. See diagram. Glue hat on head. Glue felt on back leaving one side open for photo and wood block on back of frame.

DANDY ANDY FACE PATTERN

Fold yarn strands and glue to back of head.

FLOWERY JASMINE FACE PATTERN

FLOWER PATTERNS

COWPOKE HAT BRIM PATTERN
Cut slit

Hat crown

Feather

Slit

Wood head disk

Hat brim

With hat brim point facing front, slip on head keeping slit even with top of face. Glue crown centered to back of head and feather on front of hat.

COW-POKE HAT CROWN PATTERN
Cut 1
Black Foam

Paint hair

COWPOKE FACE PATTERN

ANDY FRAME - BACK VIEW

4" Stick
3⅜"
1" small rectangles
4¾" Stick
6" Stick
4½"

Glue wood blocks for stand

ANDY FRAME - FRONT VIEW

COWPOKE ARM PATTERN

4 Rent Birdhouse & Birds

Birdhouse

MATERIALS: Paint mixing stick • 7" of 3-ply Natural jute • Woodsies: 4 small circles, 8 medium rectangles • Acrylic Paint: Buttermilk, Lamp Black, Green Mist • Drill and 3/16" drill bit • Black permanent marker

1. Paint stick, rectangles and circles. Draw details and letters with marker.

2. Assemble - Drill hole in stick. Thread jute through hole, tie lark's head knot. Glue 2 rectangles together for each roof. Glue circles, roofs and birds to stick.

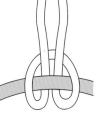

Lark's Head Knot

Blue Jay

MATERIALS: Woodsies: large teardrop, 2 medium teardrops, 2 small teardrops, medium circle, small rectangle • Acrylic Paint: True Blue, Salem Blue, Cadmium Yellow, Lamp Black, Snow White • Black permanent marker

1. Assemble wood pieces except for beak.

2. Paint bird using dry brush technique where shown. Draw eye and beak details with marker. Dot eye Lamp Black and Snow White. Glue beak on back of head.

Oriole

MATERIALS: Woodsies: large teardrop, 2 medium teardrops, small teardrop, medium circle, small rectangle • Acrylic Paint: Lamp Black, Cadmium Yellow, Snow White, Pumpkin • Black permanent marker

1. Assemble wood pieces except for beak.

2. Paint bird using dry brush technique where shown. Draw eye and beak details with marker. Dot eye Lamp Black and Snow White. Glue beak on back of head.

Cardinal

MATERIALS: Woodsies Shapes: Large teardrop, 2 medium teardrops, 2 small teardrops, medium circle, small rectangle • Black permanent marker • Acrylic Paint: Lamp Black, Cadmium Yellow, Snow White, Santa Red

1. Assemble wood pieces except for beak.

2. Paint bird using dry brush technique where shown. Draw eye and beak details with marker. Dot eye Snow White. Glue beak on back of head.

Crow

MATERIALS: Woodsies: large teardrop, 2 medium teardrops, small teardrop, medium circle, small rectangle • Acrylic Paint: Lamp Black, Cadmium Yellow, Snow White • Black permanent marker

1. Assemble wood pieces except for beak.

2. Paint bird using dry brush technique where shown. Draw eye and beak details with marker. Dot eye Snow White. Glue beak on back of head.

Painting Technique Tip:

To dry brush, dip brush in paint, dab on paper towel until almost dry then apply to project.

Bugs & Bees

Inchworm Wall Hanging

MATERIALS: 5¾" wide wood banner with 2 holes • Woodsies: medium apple, medium pumpkin • 36" of 18 gauge Gold wire • Four 9" pieces of ⅛" Green satin ribbon • Seven 13" pieces of Clear glitter round plastic lace • Two 2" pieces of Green chenille stem • 9 wood 16mm beads • 48 Green pony beads • 2 Bright Green Wikki Stix • Black permanent marker • Acrylic Paint: Cadmium Yellow, Santa Red, Pumpkin, Hot Shots Thermal Green, Hot Shots Sizzling Pink • Drill and ⅛" drill bit

1. Drill 7 evenly spaced holes in bottom edge of wood banner.

2. Paint wood pieces. Dry brush cheeks. Draw eyes and details with marker. Glue apple and pumpkin on banner.

3. Make 2 chenille inchworms and 7 plastic lace inchworms as shown in diagrams. Cut Wikki Stix into nine 2" pieces for antennae.

4. For hanger - Bend wire slightly in center and coil around pencil leaving 1" straight on ends. Shape handle, insert ends in holes, wrap to back and coil around handle. Attach piece of ribbon to hanger using lark's head knot, tie ends in overhand knot. Tie ribbon bows around hanger ribbon and each side.

Fire Fly Stand

FIRE FLY FACE PATTERN

MATERIALS: 1¼" x 1⅜" diameter wood apple • Doll pin stand • ⅜" x 1¾" craft disk • Craft pick • Mini spring clothespin • Woodsies: 2 large teardrops, 2 medium teardrops, large pumpkin • 2 Ruby 4mm acrylic cabochons • 6" of Orange Wikki Stix • Three 12" strands of raffia • Acrylic Paint: Bright Green, Lamp Black, Cadmium Yellow, Cherry Red, Hot Shots Torrid Orange, Hot Shots Fiery Red • Black and Pink textile marker • Acrylic spray sealer

1. Paint wood pieces. Dry brush edges as shown. Blush cheeks with Pink marker. Draw details with Black marker.

2. Assemble pieces and glue in place. Glue clothespin. Wrap raffia around stem, tie bow. Fold Wikki Stix in half, press folded end on back side of head for antenna.

Fruit Fly Stand

MATERIALS: 1¼" x 1⅜" wood apple • Doll pin stand • ⅜" x 1¾" craft disk • Craft pick • Mini spring clothespin • Woodsies: 2 medium teardrops, medium oval, 2 small teardrops • Acrylic cabochons: 2 Black 10mm x 7mm pear, 2 Emerald 8mm x 4mm navette, 4 Ruby 4mm • 2" of Neon Pink plastic craft lace • Three 12" strands of raffia • Acrylic Paint: Bright Green, Lamp Black, Wisteria, Hot Shots Torrid Orange • Black and Pink textile markers • Acrylic spray sealer

1. Paint wood pieces. Blush cheeks with Pink marker. Draw details with Black marker.

2. Assemble pieces and glue in place. Glue clothespin extending ⅛" above top of disk. Wrap raffia around stem, tie bow. Glue cabochons on face, wings and body. Fold plastic lace in half, press folded end under the back side of the head.

Make 2 - Chenille Inchworms

Fold Wikki Stix in half for antenna. Insert in bead and glue.

Glue chenille stem in large wood bead, add pony beads and glue bottom of stem to back of banner.

Front of wood banner

Fold lace in half, insert into hole and pull lace ends through loop to make lark's head knot.

Make 7 - Lace Inchworms

Wood banner

Lark's head knot

Insert folded Wikki Stix in wood bead hole and glue.

Tie overhand knot in lace.

Glue cabochon eyes

Glue clothespin to back of disk body.

Craft pick

LADYBUG FACE PATTERN

Ladybug Stand

MATERIALS: 1¼" x 1⅜" wood apple • Doll pin stand • ⅜" x 1¾" craft disk • Craft pick • Mini spring clothespin • 9 Black 5mm and 2 Green 4mm x 6mm acrylic cabochons • Woodsies: 2 large teardrops, 2 medium teardrops, medium apple • Three 12" strands of raffia • Acrylic Paint: Bright Green, Cherry Red, Cadmium Yellow, Flesh Tone, Lamp Black • Acrylic spray sealer • Black and Pink textile markers

1. Paint wood pieces. Blush cheeks with Pink marker. Draw details with Black marker.

2. Assemble pieces and glue in place. Glue closed end of clothespin even with top edge of disk. Wrap raffia around stem, tie bow. Glue on wings, body and eyes.

Bugs & Bees

Yellow Jacket

MATERIALS: Craft spoon • Woodsies: small teardrop, 4 medium teardrops, large teardrop, 2 medium rectangles • Acrylic Paint: Cadmium Yellow, Buttermilk, Lamp Black, Flesh Tone, Santa Red • Black and Pink textile markers

1. Paint wood pieces. Transfer face pattern. Blush cheeks with Pink marker. Draw details with Black marker.

2. Assemble pieces and glue in place.

BACK VIEW ASSEMBLY DIAGRAM

Medium Teardrop

Large Teardrop

Medium Rectangle

Craft Spoon

Small Teardrop

YELLOW JACKET FACE PATTERN

Cricket

MATERIALS: Craft spoon • 4 craft picks • Woodsies: large egg, small teardrop, 3 medium teardrops, medium oval, medium rectangle, small circle • Acrylic Paint: Lamp Black, Soft Peach, Toffee, Tangelo Orange, Yellow Green, Mink Tan, Snow White, Spice Pink • Black permanent marker • Hot glue and glue gun

1. Cut craft picks for legs. Paint pieces.

2. Transfer patterns. Dry brush as shown. Blush cheeks with Spice Pink. Draw details with Black marker.

3. Assemble pieces and glue in place. Mound a small blob of hot glue on bottom of each foot. Let dry.

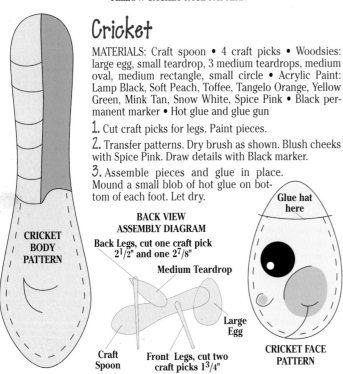

CRICKET BODY PATTERN

BACK VIEW ASSEMBLY DIAGRAM

Back Legs, cut one craft pick 2½" and one 2⅞"

Medium Teardrop

Large Egg

Craft Spoon

Front Legs, cut two craft picks 1¾"

Glue hat here

CRICKET FACE PATTERN

Bumble Bee

MATERIALS: Woodsies: large apple, medium pumpkin, 2 large light bulbs, 1½" piece off pointed end of craft pick • 3" of Black Wikki Stix • 2 Red 4mm acrylic cabochons • Acrylic Paint: Cadmium Yellow, Lamp Black, Buttermilk, Soft Peach • Acrylic spray sealer • Black and Pink textile markers

1. Paint wood pieces. Blush cheeks with Pink marker. Draw details with Black marker.

2. Assemble pieces and glue in place. Fold Wikki Stix in half, press on back of head for antennae.

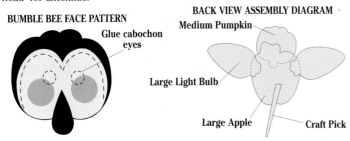

BUMBLE BEE FACE PATTERN

Glue cabochon eyes

BACK VIEW ASSEMBLY DIAGRAM

Medium Pumpkin

Large Light Bulb

Large Apple

Craft Pick

Horse Fly

MATERIALS: Woodsies: 4 large teardrops, 2 medium teardrops, medium oval, small octagon, 2 small circles • Acrylic Paint: Antique Teal, Lamp Black, Snow White, Dazzling Metallics Glorious Gold • 6", 4¼", 4" and 3" pieces of Wikki Stix

1. Paint wood pieces. Dry brush as shown.

2. Assemble pieces and glue in place. Glue wings on body slightly angled. Fold 3" Wikki Stix, press on back of head for antenna. Shape Wikki Stix pieces and press legs on body.

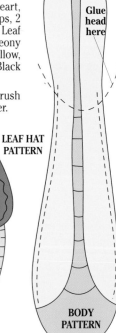

BODY PATTERN

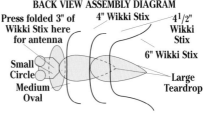

BACK VIEW ASSEMBLY DIAGRAM

Press folded 3" of Wikki Stix here for antenna

4" Wikki Stix

4½" Wikki Stix

6" Wikki Stix

Small Circle

Medium Oval

Large Teardrop

Don't Bug Me

MATERIALS: Unfinished door hanger • Craft spoon • 5 craft picks • Woodsies: Large egg, medium heart, 2 small circles, medium circle, 2 small teardrops, 2 small candy corn, 7 small ovals • Acrylic Paint: Leaf Green, Buttermilk, Lamp Black, Snow White, Peony Pink, Spice Pink, Tangelo Orange, Cadmium Yellow, Yellow Green, Dark Turquoise, Soft Peach • Black permanent marker • Yellow pony bead

1. Paint wood pieces. Transfer patterns. Dry brush edges as shown. Draw details with Black marker.

2. Assemble and glue flower pieces together, glue to hanger. Assemble pieces for head and body, glue.

3. For back legs, cut 2½" off pointed end of 2 picks, cut rounded end 1" long for 2 arms. For front legs, cut 3" off rounded end of 2 picks. Glue legs together as shown. Glue feet on legs and arms on legs. Glue 1 small oval to top back of spoon body and 1 small circle to back bottom of body for support. Glue bug on door hanger.

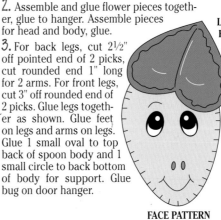

Glue head here

LEAF HAT PATTERN

BODY PATTERN

FACE PATTERN

Little Bookworm

BOOKWORM FACE PATTERN

MATERIALS: Jumbo craft stick • 7 medium circle Woodsies • Acrylic Paint: Yellow Green, Lamp Black, Hot Shots Scorching Yellow • 1½" of Black plastic lace • Black and Pink textile markers

1. Paint wood pieces.

2. Glue circles together as shown. Glue caterpillar on front of craft stick. Blush cheeks with Pink marker. Draw details with Black marker. Glue plastic lace to back of head and cut down middle for antennae.

Grasshopper
Instructions & patterns are on page 16.

Orange Bug

MATERIALS: Woodsies: medium egg, medium teardrop, large teardrop, small oval, 2 medium ovals, 2 small circles • 7", 4½" and 4" pieces of Black Wikki Stix • Acrylic Paint: Tangelo Orange, Cadmium Yellow, Lamp Black, Snow White • Black permanent marker

1. Paint wood pieces. Dry brush edges as shown. Draw details with marker.

2. Assemble pieces and glue in place. Fold 4" Wikki Stix in half, press on back of nose for antennae. Bend remaining Wikki Stix pieces and press in place for legs.

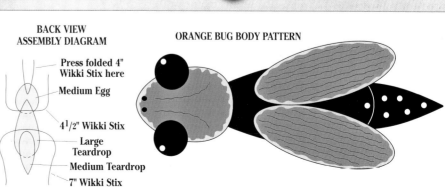

BACK VIEW ASSEMBLY DIAGRAM

- Press folded 4" Wikki Stix here
- Medium Egg
- 4½" Wikki Stix
- Large Teardrop
- Medium Teardrop
- 7" Wikki Stix

ORANGE BUG BODY PATTERN

Noah's Ark Wall Hanging

Begin Here

1a. ARK BOTTOM - BACK VIEW
Middle Section

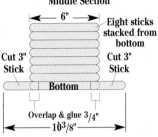

6"

Eight sticks stacked from bottom

Cut 3" Stick

Cut 3" Stick

Bottom

Overlap & glue 3/4"

$10^3/8$"

1b. ARK BOTTOM - BACK VIEW
End Sections

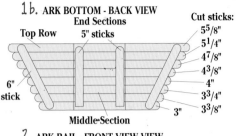

Top Row
5" sticks

6" stick

Middle Section

Cut sticks:
$5^5/8$"
$5^1/4$"
$4^7/8$"
$4^3/8$"
4"
$3^3/4$"
$3^3/8$"
3"

2. ARK RAIL - FRONT VIEW VIEW
Make same as top row of ark bottom.

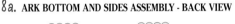

3. ARK SIDES - BACK VIEW
Make 2

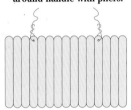

Cut $2^1/2$"

6"

6"

4. ARK TOP - BACK VIEW
Drill 1/8" holes 1/4" from edge.

6"

5"   5"

6"

$1^1/2$"

2"

5. ARK ROOF - BACK VIEW
Assemble 12 full sticks, secure with 4 cut pieces.

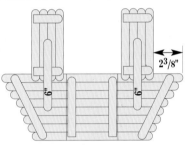

$3^1/2$" $3^1/2$"

$2^1/2$" $2^1/2$"

ARK ROOF - FRONT VIEW

$11^3/4$"

$13^3/4$"
$15^3/4$"
$16^3/4$"

6. PAINT ARK

7. MAKE HANGER - FRONT VIEW
Coil wire. Insert ends of wire through holes in top of ark. Twist ends back around handle with pliers.

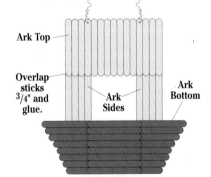

8a. ARK BOTTOM AND SIDES ASSEMBLY - BACK VIEW

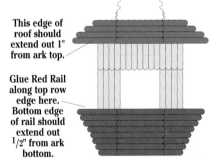

$2^3/8$"

6"   6"

8b. ARK SIDE & TOP ASSEMBLY - FRONT VIEW

Ark Top

Overlap sticks 3/4" and glue.

Ark Sides

Ark Bottom

8c. ARK ROOF & RAIL ASSEMBLY - FRONT VIEW
Glue top of roof edge to top of ark edge at an angle.

This edge of roof should extend out 1" from ark top.

Glue Red Rail along top row edge here. Bottom edge of rail should extend out 1/2" from ark bottom.

FROG PATTERN
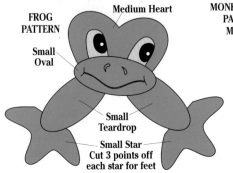

Medium Heart

Small Oval

Small Teardrop

Small Star
Cut 3 points off each star for feet

MONKEY FACE PATTERN
Make 2
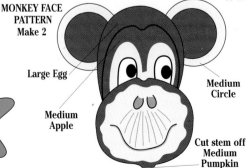

Large Egg

Medium Apple

Medium Circle

Cut stem off Medium Pumpkin

CAMEL FACE PATTERN
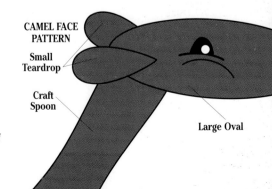

Small Teardrop

Craft Spoon

Large Oval

Noah's Ark

MATERIALS: 77 jumbo craft sticks • 12 craft spoons • 2 wood $1^1/2$" x 1/8" disks • Woodsies: 5 large and 2 medium hearts, 2 medium and 2 small stars, 6 small circles, large teardrop, 5 medium teardrops, 16 small teardrops, 4 large ovals, 8 small ovals, 2 large eggs, 2 medium apples, 2 medium pumpkins, large and small candy corn, 2 medium wings • One 15" and five 6" pieces of 18 gauge galvanized wire • 24" of 3-ply jute • Acrylic Paint: Williamsburg Blue, Santa Red, Bittersweet Chocolate, Soft Peach, Cadmium Yellow, Milk Chocolate, Lamp Black, Snow White, Slate Grey, Camel, French Mauve, Buttermilk, Bright Green, Yellow Green • Acrylic gloss spray sealer • Deco Art Oak gel stain • Black and Pink textile markers • Brown bumpy chenille stem, cut in half • Glue • Scissors • Pliers • Craft snips • Ruler • Drill and 1/8" bit

1. **Bottom of Ark.** Cut, assemble and glue craft sticks.

2. **Rail.** Glue 3 sticks together in the same length and manner as the top row of ark bottom. Set aside.

3. **Sides of Ark.** Cut, assemble and glue craft sticks.

4. **Top.** Cut, assemble and glue craft sticks.

5. **Roof.** Cut, assemble and glue craft sticks.

6. **Paint Ark.** Write RAIN-RAIN GO AWAY on banner with Black marker. Spray with sealer. Let dry.

7. **Hanger.** Coil ends of wire around pencil. Shape hanger, insert ends of wire through holes in top of ark, twist ends back around handle with pliers.

8. **Assemble.** Place bottom of ark face down on flat surface. Glue sides to top. Center and glue one stick on each side of ark. Turn ark to front. Glue top edge of roof on top edge of ark at an angle. Bottom edge should extend out 1". Glue rail on top edge of bottom in same manner with bottom edge extending 1/2". Coil jute to form lasso, glue lasso, hearts and stars in place on ark.

Ark Animals

Paint as shown. Assemble and glue wood pieces together. Draw details with Black marker. Let dry. Spray with sealer. Glue in place as shown.

Frog. Cut 3 points off each star for feet.

Monkey. Trace and transfer pattern for face. Dry brush where shown. Turn under 1/4" on each tip of chenille stems with pliers. Glue arms centered on back of each monkey.

Camel. Transfer pattern. Dry brush where shown.

Giraffe. Transfer pattern. Dry brush edges and spots.

Elephant. Coil 6" of wire around pencil. Glue one end of wire to back of head. Set aside.

Zebra. Transfer pattern. Attach wire as for Elephant.

Burro. Dry brush where shown. Attach wire as for elephant.

Dove. Transfer pattern. Dry brush head, wings back and tail. Paint beak add details. Glue beak on back of head last.

Caterpillar. Glue small circles together. Paint cheeks with Pink marker.

Complete Animals. Position animals as shown. Glue end of springs, bottoms of giraffes and camel to back of ark. Position arms and glue each monkey, caterpillar, frog and dove to front. Glue banner to front on opposite ends of hanger.

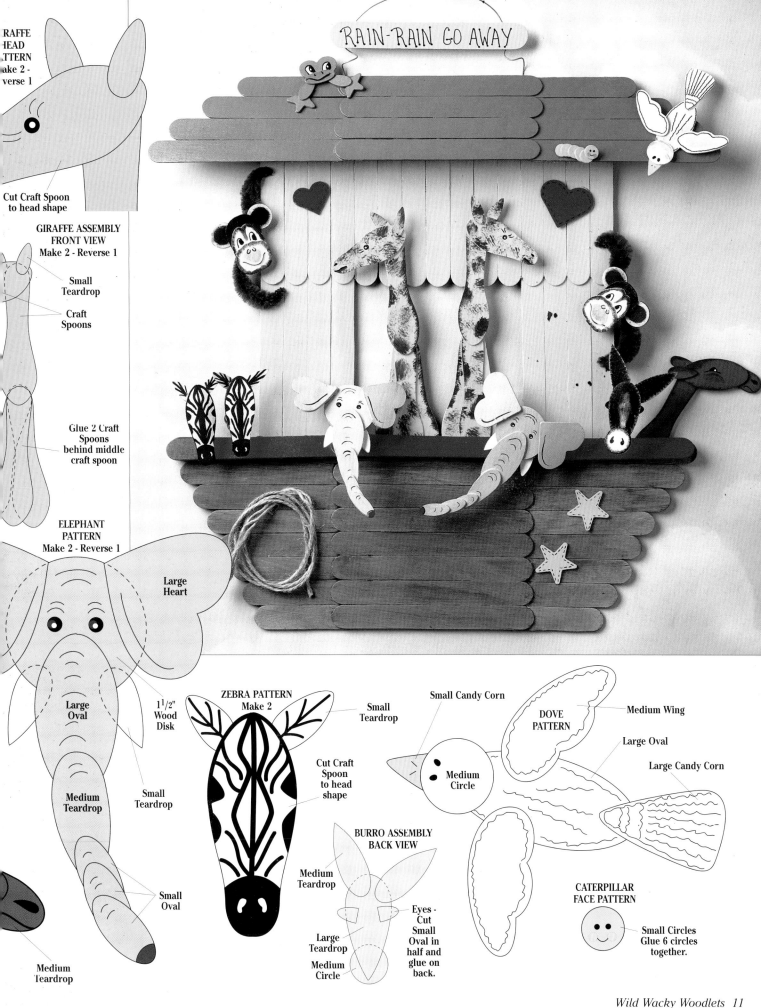

GIRAFFE
HEAD
PATTERN
Make 2 -
Reverse 1

Cut Craft Spoon
to head shape

GIRAFFE ASSEMBLY
FRONT VIEW
Make 2 - Reverse 1

Small
Teardrop

Craft
Spoons

Glue 2 Craft
Spoons
behind middle
craft spoon

ELEPHANT
PATTERN
Make 2 - Reverse 1

Large
Heart

Large
Oval

1¹/₂"
Wood
Disk

Medium
Teardrop

Small
Teardrop

Small
Oval

Medium
Teardrop

RAIN-RAIN GO AWAY

ZEBRA PATTERN
Make 2

Small
Teardrop

Cut Craft
Spoon
to head
shape

BURRO ASSEMBLY
BACK VIEW

Medium
Teardrop

Eyes -
Cut
Small
Oval in
half and
glue on
back.

Large
Teardrop

Medium
Circle

Small Candy Corn

DOVE
PATTERN

Medium
Circle

Medium Wing

Large Oval

Large Candy Corn

CATERPILLAR
FACE PATTERN

Small Circles
Glue 6 circles
together.

Animal Frames

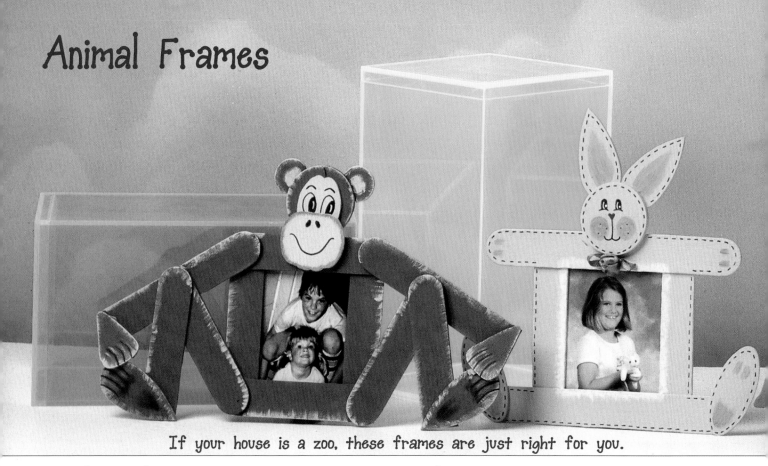

If your house is a zoo, these frames are just right for you.

Funky Monkey

MATERIALS: 1½" x ⅛" flat wood disk • 10 jumbo craft sticks • 1 craft stick • Woodsies: 2 large pumpkins, medium apple, 2 small circles, 2 large candy corn, 2 large teardrops • ¾" wood block • 3⅛" x 3⅝" piece of felt • Acrylic Paint: Milk Chocolate, Toffee, Lamp Black • Black permanent marker • Acrylic spray sealer

1. Cut craft sticks for frame and assemble. See diagram.

2. Paint frame and wood pieces. Dry brush as shown.

3. Glue wood pieces together and glue to frame. See face pattern. Glue felt on back of frame leaving one side open for photo and wood block on back of frame for stand.

Pinky Bunny

MATERIALS: 1½" x ⅛" flat wood disk • Woodsies: 2 large teardrops, 2 large ovals, 4 small rectangles • 4 jumbo craft sticks • ¾" wood block • Acrylic Paint: Snow White, Baby Pink, Boysenberry Pink, Santa Red • 3⅝" x 3¾" piece of felt • ⅜" Red satin rose with Green ribbon leaves • Black permanent marker • Acrylic spray sealer

1. Make basic frame.

2. Paint frame and wood pieces.

3. Glue wood pieces on frame. Draw broken line ⅛" from edge with marker. Make Dip Dot heart nose. Dry brush inner edge of frame.

4. Glue ribbon below chin and felt on back side leaving one side open for photo. Glue wood block to back of frame for stand.

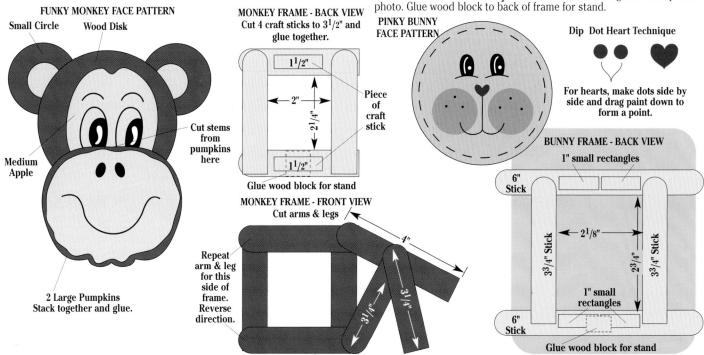

FUNKY MONKEY FACE PATTERN

Small Circle Wood Disk

Medium Apple

2 Large Pumpkins Stack together and glue.

MONKEY FRAME - BACK VIEW
Cut 4 craft sticks to 3½" and glue together.

1½"

2"

2¼"

Piece of craft stick

Cut stems from pumpkins here

1½"

Glue wood block for stand

MONKEY FRAME - FRONT VIEW
Cut arms & legs

Repeat arm & leg for this side of frame. Reverse direction.

4"

3¼"

3¼"

¾"

PINKY BUNNY FACE PATTERN

Dip Dot Heart Technique

For hearts, make dots side by side and drag paint down to form a point.

BUNNY FRAME - BACK VIEW

1" small rectangles

6" Stick

3¾" Stick

2⅛"

2¾"

3¾" Stick

1" small rectangles

6" Stick

Glue wood block for stand

Funny Frog

MATERIALS: 6 jumbo craft sticks • Woodsies: large heart, 6 large ovals, 6 large ghosts • ³/₄" wood block • Two 15mm wiggle eyes • Acrylic Paint: Bright Green, Hot Shots Thermal Green • Mosaic Crackle Medium Step #1, Mosaic Crackle Activator Step #2 • 3¼" x 4" piece of felt • Black permanent marker

1. Cut craft sticks for frame and assemble. See diagram. Stack and glue 2 ghosts together for back feet. Stack and glue 2 large ovals together for snout.

2. Paint assembled frame (mix 2 parts of Crackle Medium Step #1 to one part Bright Green paint, let dry 30 minutes). Paint front side of frame with a thin to medium coat of Thermal Green. When dry, brush a heavy coat of Crackle Activator Step #2 over front surface of frame. Let dry. Crackles will appear as activator dries.

3. Glue eyes on face. Cut felt to fit, glue on back of frame leaving one side open for photo. Glue wood block centered on back ³/₁₆" above bottom edge of frame.

Clara Cow

MATERIALS: 2 craft sticks • 10 jumbo craft sticks • Woodsies: 2 medium teardrops, large teardrop, large heart (udder) • Acrylic Paint: Lamp Black, Snow White, Baby Pink • Two 15mm wiggle eyes • 1" copper cow bell • 12" of ¼" Red satin ribbon • 18" of 18 gauge Icy copper wire • 4⅝" x 5⅝" piece of felt • Black permanent marker

1. Make basic frame. Assemble cow head. Make hooves. See diagrams. Tail - Cut 3½" off one end of craft stick, glue to back of large teardrop.

2. Paint frame and wood pieces. Load brush with equal parts of Baby Pink and Snow White to paint snout. Dry brush tip of tail Grey (mix dab of Lamp Black with Snow White to make Grey).

3. Glue eyes on face, hooves on legs, tail and udder on back of frame. Tie ribbon around frame below snout, string bell and tie bow. Glue felt on back of frame leaving one side open for photo. Coil wire around pencil. Shape handle, glue ends on back of frame.

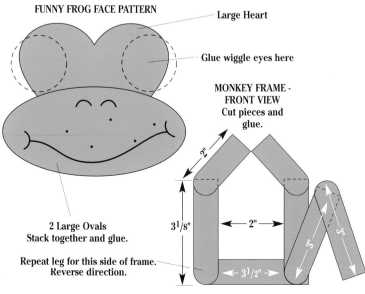

FUNNY FROG FACE PATTERN

Large Heart

Glue wiggle eyes here

**MONKEY FRAME -
FRONT VIEW**
Cut pieces and glue.

2"

2 Large Ovals
Stack together and glue.

Repeat leg for this side of frame.
Reverse direction.

3⅛"

2"

3½"

3"

3"

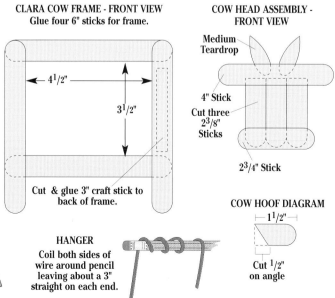

CLARA COW FRAME - FRONT VIEW
Glue four 6" sticks for frame.

4½"

3½"

Cut & glue 3" craft stick to back of frame.

HANGER
Coil both sides of wire around pencil leaving about a 3" straight on each end.

**COW HEAD ASSEMBLY -
FRONT VIEW**

Medium
Teardrop

4" Stick

Cut three
2³/₈"
Sticks

2³/₄" Stick

COW HOOF DIAGRAM

1½"

Cut ½"
on angle

Croaking frogs... cawing crows... these mobiles
are color in motion.

Fun Frogs, Crows & Parrot Mobiles

Fun Frogs

MATERIALS: Woodsies: large heart, 8 medium hearts, 7 small hearts, 5 medium ovals, 21 small ovals, 2 small circles • 12" wood ruler • One 13", one 12" and two 10" pieces of 1/8" Green satin ribbon • 24 assorted heart pony beads • Acrylic Paint: Bright Green, Yellow Green, Lamp Black, Snow White, Santa Red, Cadmium Yellow • Drill and 1/8" drill bit • Black permanent marker

1. Assemble frogs and glue. Omit wood eyes on large frog for now.

2. Paint frogs. Draw details with marker. Paint and glue eyes on large frog.

3. Cut ruler at 8". Drill holes in corners and 3/8" above bottom as shown. Thread ribbon through front corner holes and tie knots in back to secure. Attach remaining ribbons to bottom of ruler in same manner. Glue baby frogs on ribbons. String and glue 8 beads on each ribbon.

Baby Crows

MATERIALS: Woodsies: 7 medium octagons, 7 medium circles, 7 small hearts, 14 small teardrops • 3" brass ring • 12" and two 20" pieces of 1/8" Yellow ribbon • Eight 4" feathers • 8 Yellow and 8 Red pony beads • 4 Black and 8 Orange oval pony beads • Acrylic Paint: Lamp Black, Cadmium Yellow • Black permanent marker

1. Assemble crows and glue. Omit beaks.

2. Paint crows. Draw details with marker. Paint and glue beaks on heads.

3. Glue crows on ring. For hanger, fold 12" ribbon in half and tie on ring using lark's head knot. Tie ends in overhand knot. Fold remaining ribbons in half and lark's head knot on bottom of ring. String beads. Knot ribbon below beads. Insert and glue feathers into each string of beads.

Parrot Mandella

MATERIALS: 3" brass ring • Six 16" pieces of White leather lace • Woodsies: medium candy corn, large pumpkin, 2 small apples, 2 small circles, 4 large teardrops • Craft spoon • 20 Green, 20 Yellow, 20 Orange, and 10 Dark Turquoise pony beads • 10 Orange feathers • Acrylic Paint: Leaf Green, Pumpkin, Cadmium Yellow, Lamp Black, Snow White

1. For hanger, fold one leather strip in half and tie on ring using lark's head knot. Tie ends in overhand knot. Fold remaining leather pieces, do not tie ends, attach in same manner to bottom of ring. String beads. Vary bead positions leaving 1" to 2" of leather below beads. Insert one feather in each string of beads. Glue.

2. Paint wood pieces. Dry brush head and tail where shown.

3. Assemble wood pieces and glue. Glue craft spoon on back of lace on brass ring and wings on spoon and front side of leather lace.

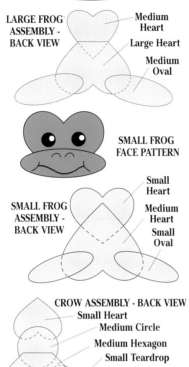

LARGE FROG FACE PATTERN

LARGE FROG ASSEMBLY - BACK VIEW
- Medium Heart
- Large Heart
- Medium Oval

SMALL FROG FACE PATTERN

SMALL FROG ASSEMBLY - BACK VIEW
- Small Heart
- Medium Heart
- Small Oval

CROW ASSEMBLY - BACK VIEW
- Small Heart
- Medium Circle
- Medium Hexagon
- Small Teardrop

CROW HEAD PATTERN

Lark's Head Knot

PARROT BODY ASSEMBLY - FRONT VIEW
- Large Pumpkin
- Craft Spoon
- Large Teardrops

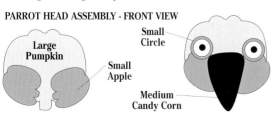

PARROT HEAD ASSEMBLY - FRONT VIEW
- Large Pumpkin
- Small Circle
- Small Apple
- Medium Candy Corn

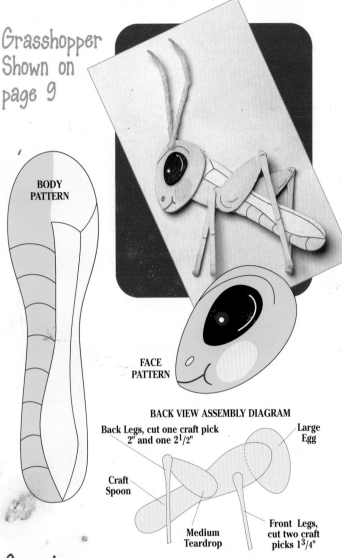

Grasshopper Shown on page 9

BODY PATTERN

FACE PATTERN

BACK VIEW ASSEMBLY DIAGRAM

Back Legs, cut one craft pick 2" and one 2¹/₂"

Large Egg

Craft Spoon

Medium Teardrop

Front Legs, cut two craft picks 1³/₄"

Grasshopper

MATERIALS: Craft spoon • 4 craft picks • Woodsies: large egg, small egg, 2 medium teardrops • Two 2" pieces of White Wikki Stix • Acrylic Paint: Yellow Green, Black Forest Green, Limeade, Santa Red, Snow White, Spice Pink • Black permanent marker • Hot glue and glue gun

1. Cut craft picks for legs. Paint pieces.

2. Transfer patterns. Second coat top portion of grasshopper. Second coat all remaining body pieces. Blush cheeks with Spice Pink. Draw details with Black marker.

3. Assemble pieces and glue in place. Mound a small blob of hot glue on bottom of each foot. Let dry. Press a Wikki Stix on each side of head for antennae.

Now I Lay Me down to Sleep

MATERIALS: Wood slat sign • 2¹/₂" craft disk, • Woodsies: small heart, 2 medium hearts, 3 large circles • 24" of 18 gauge copper wire • Acrylic Paint: Dark Turquoise, Spice Pink, Leaf Green, Soft Peach, Pink Chiffon, Cashmere Beige • Pink and Black textile markers • 12" of ¹/₄" Light Turquoise satin picot ribbon • Drill and ¹/₈" drill bit • Fine grade sandpaper • Acrylic spray sealer

1. Drill holes in top corners of wood slat sign. Sand smooth.

2. Paint wood pieces. Dry brush sky, grass and other areas as shown. Blush cheeks with Pink marker. Draw details and words with Black marker.

3. Coil wire, shape hanging loop, insert ends of wire through holes and bend back around hanger with pliers.

4. Assemble and glue bear pieces together. Glue bear and hearts on slat sign. Tie bow. Glue on bear.

Morning & Evening Signs

Smile, Bee Happy

MATERIALS: Wood slat sign • 2¹/₂" craft disk • 32 craft picks. • Woodsies: 2 small hearts, medium heart, 2 small teardrops, medium teardrop • 24" of 18 gauge copper wire • Acrylic Paint: Cadmium Yellow, Snow White, Santa Red, Lamp Black, Gingerbread • Pink and Black textile markers • Acrylic spray sealer

1. Glue craft picks to flat side of craft disk.

2. Paint wood pieces. Dry brush where shown. Blush cheeks with Pink marker. Draw details and words with Black marker.

3. Glue bees pieces to front of sign as shown. Bee tongue is painted in black. Glue hearts in place.

4. For hanger, coil wire around pencil. Shape hanger offsetting loops to balance slat sign. Glue ends of wire on side edges of wood slat.

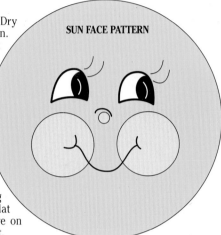

SUN FACE PATTERN

SMILE BE HAPPY

WORDS & BEE PATTERNS

Medium Heart Head

Medium Teardrop Body

Tongue is painted on sign.

Glue Large Circle to back of head.

Large Circle

BEAR FACE/HEAD PATTERN Wood Disk

Large Circle

"SMILE" BE HAPPY

Now I Lay Me Down to Sleep...

Little signs remind us to be happy or sleep peacefully.

Now I Lay Me Down to Sleep...

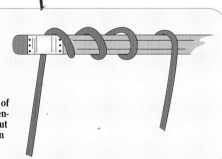
To Make Wire Handles

Coil both sides of wire around pencil leaving about a 3" straight on each end.

Animal Frames

Walk on the wild side...
these frames bring out
the animal in you.

LION FORELOCK PATTERN
Cut 1
Brown Foam

LION HALF MANE PATTERN
Cut 1
Brown Foam

LION EAR PATTERN
Cut 2 Brown Foam
Paint Golden Straw

Gerry Giraffe

MATERIALS: 1¾" craft disk • 5 jumbo craft sticks • Woodsies: large egg, 2 small ovals • 2 craft picks • Two 1½" wood blocks • Acrylic Paint: Cadmium Yellow, Lamp Black, Snow White, Gingerbread • 12" of Red ¾" satin ribbon • Two 3" strands of 3-ply jute • 6" square of Yellow felt • Black permanent marker

1. Cut craft sticks for frame and assemble. See diagram. For horns, cut 1⅛" off rounded ends of 2 craft picks. Glue muzzle on front of head, ears and horns on back of head.

2. Paint frame and wood pieces. Sponge on spots and dry brush all edges and center of face.

3. Glue head and tail on frame. Cut felt to fit, glue on back of frame. Glue 2 wood blocks centered on back frame ³⁄₁₆" above bottom edge.

5" Stick

4¼"

9"

GIRAFFE BODY - FRONT VIEW

4¾"

6"

Leo Lion

MATERIALS: 1½" x ⅛" flat wood disk • Woodsies: 2 large candy corn, small heart, 4 small rectangles • 4 jumbo craft sticks • ¾" wood block • Acrylic Paint: Golden Straw, Milk Chocolate, Snow White, Lamp Black • ¼" Black pompom • 6" x 3" piece of Brown craft foam • 6" Brown chenille stem • 6" of 3-ply Natural jute • 3⅝" x 4" piece of felt • Black permanent marker • Acrylic spray sealer

1. Make basic frame on page 2. For feet, shape heels by cutting off both corners on straight end of scraps left from sides. Transfer patterns, cut out mane and ear pieces from foam. Glue paws and feet to frame.

2. Paint frame and wood pieces. Dry brush streaks where shown.

3. Glue nose on snout, snout and forelock on face and head and ears on full mane. Glue full mane on arms, half mane centered on full mane with straight edge resting on top edge of arms and felt on back of frame leaving one side open for photo. Glue wood block centered on back frame ³⁄₁₆" above bottom edge. For tail, fold chenille stem in

half over center of jute, twist chenille stem tightly to ends. Glue tail on back of frame.

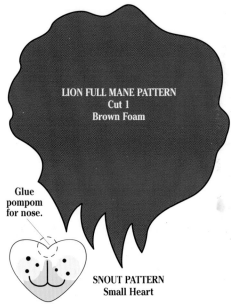

LION FULL MANE PATTERN
Cut 1
Brown Foam

Glue pompom for nose.

SNOUT PATTERN
Small Heart